HOPE AND FEAR BALANCED

HOPE AND FEAR BALANCED

In a Sermon Preached at the Tuesday
Lecture, at Salters Hall, July 24TH, 1711

❧

REV. MATTHEW HENRY

MINISTER OF THE GOSPEL IN CHESTER

CURIOSMITH

MINNEAPOLIS

Published by Curiosmith.
Minneapolis, Minnesota.
Internet: curiosmith.com.

The text of this edition is from *The Miscellaneous Works of the Rev. Matthew Henry*, published by ROBERT CARTER & BROTHERS, 1855.

Scripture quotations designated (NIV) are from the Holy Bible, NEW INTERNATIONAL VERSION®. Copyright © 1973, 1978, 1984 by Biblica, Inc. All rights reserved worldwide. Used by permission.

The "Guide to the Contents" was added to this edition by the publisher.

Supplementary content and cover design:
Copyright © 2017 Charles J. Doe.

ISBN 9781946145154

GUIDE TO THE CONTENTS
———∘∘⦂⊙⦂∘∘———

HOPE AND FEAR BALANCED

The Lord taketh pleasure in them that fear him, in those that hope in his mercy.—PSALM 147:11.

The dignity and privilege of the righteous, who are God's favorites, here appear bright and blessed, very blessed, very bright; and to an eye of faith, the luster of them far exceeds even that of crowns and coronets; though their honor like their life is hidden,[1] and, therefore, the world knows them not.[2] What can prove them more great, what more happy, than this, that the God of heaven *takes pleasure* in them?

That God should be *at peace* with any of the children of men, (that degenerate, guilty, and obnoxious race,) is more than we could have expected, considering his justice and holiness; but that he should *take pleasure* in them, should set

---

1 Colossians 3:3.
2 1 John 3:1.

them apart for himself,[1] gather them in his arms, carry them in his bosom,[2] value them as his peculiar treasure, and make them up as his jewels;[3] this is that which eternity itself will be little enough, and short enough, to be spent in the thankful admiration of. *Lord, what is man that thou shouldst thus magnify him, and set thine heart upon him?*

God takes pleasure in his saints, that is, in his own image upon them: *he rejoiceth in the work of his own hands.*[4] Not that God is capable of receiving any addition to the infinite complacency he takes in himself, and in his own perfections, from any creature; but thus he is pleased to express the favor he bears to his chosen.[5] He *delights not in the strength of a horse,* (so it is said in the foregoing verse,) he *taketh not pleasure in the legs of a man.*[6] Princes and great men take delight in these, both for their entertainment, they divert themselves with horse races and foot races, and for their service, they make use of horse guards and foot guards, bring into the field squadrons of horse and battalions of foot, and review their troops with a great deal of satisfaction. But does God do so? No, *he takes pleasure in them*

---

1 Psalm 4:3.
2 Isaiah 40:11.
3 Malachi 3:17.
4 Psalm 104:31.
5 Psalm 106:4, 5.
6 Psalm 147:10.

that fear him: he *delights to behold the righteous,*[1] delights to converse with them, invites them into fellowship with himself, and with them his secret is. He delights to employ them, and makes them the instruments of his glory: and herein he magnifies himself, that he has *pleasure in the prosperity of his servants.*[2]

But the CHARACTER here given of God's favorites is THAT for the sake of which I chose this text, and which I shall speak more largely to. They are such as both *fear God,* and *hope in his mercy.* The fear of God I know is often put for all religion; but it being here distinguished from a hope in his mercy, I choose rather to understand it in a more limited sense, as signifying a dread of his majesty.

Fear and hope are passions of the mind so contrary the one to the other, that, with regard to the same object, it is strange they should meet in the same laudable character: yet here we see they do so, and it is the praise of the same persons, that they both fear God, and hope in him.

Whence we may gather this doctrine:

That in every concern that lies upon our hearts, we should still endeavor to keep the balance even between hope and fear.

We know how much the health of the body

---

1 Psalm 11:7.
2 Psalm 35:27.

depends upon a due temperament of the humors, such as preserves any one from being predominant above the rest; and how much the safety and peace of the nations result from a *due* balance of trade and power, that no one grow too great for its neighbors: and, so necessary is it to the health and welfare of our souls, that there be a due proportion maintained between their powers and passions, and that the one may always be a check upon the other, to keep it from running into extremes; as in these affections mentioned in the text. A holy fear of God must be a check upon our hope, to keep that from swelling into presumption; and a pious hope in God must be a check upon our fear, to keep that from sinking into despondency.

This balance must, I say, by a wise and steady hand, be kept even in every concern that lies upon our hearts, and that we have thoughts about. I shall enumerate those that are of greatest importance.

We must keep up both hope and fear,

I. As to the concerns of our souls, and our spiritual and eternal state.

II. As to our outward concerns, relating to the body, and the life that now is.

III. As to the public concerns of the church of God, and our own land and nation.

In reference to each of these, we must always study and strive to support that affection, whether it be hope or fear, which the present temper of our minds and circumstances of our case make necessary to preserve us from an extreme.

I. Nothing certainly does so much *concern* us, and ought to lie so *near our hearts*, as the *prosperity of our souls*, and their happiness in the favor of God, and their fitness to serve him here, and enjoy him for ever. This certainly ought to be the chief and continual care of every man in this life, to approve himself to an eternal God above him, and to prepare himself for an everlasting state before him. This is the concern of the *better part*, and is of all other the most weighty concern. Now, for the due managing of this concern, it is requisite that we *take our work before us*, and give each part of it its place and due proportion, so as that one devout affection may not intrench upon and exclude another. As the beauty of God's being consists in the harmony of his attributes, so the beauty of his image on our souls consists in the harmony of our graces, and the concurrence of them all to the maintaining of our due subjection to God, and due government of ourselves.

In eternity there is neither hope nor fear. In heaven they are both lost in an endless fruition: glorified saints, as they are for ever *quiet from the fear of evil*, and out of the reach of it, so they have nothing more or better to hope for, than what they are already entered into the enjoyment of; *and what a man sees, why doth he yet hope for?*[1] In hell they are

1 Romans 8:24.

both lost in an endless despair: they have nothing
to fear there, where they know the worst, and must
feel to eternity what they would not *fear;* nor have
they any thing to hope for, when the door of mercy
is shut against them, and a great gulf fixed between
them and all blessedness, never to be removed. But
in our present state, there is and must be a mixture
both of hope and fear; and we must keep up our
communion with God, and do our duty to him by
the seasonable exercises of both: and thus we must
sing both of mercy and judgment, and *sing unto
God* of both.[1]

1. We must keep up both *a holy dread of God,
and a humble delight in him;* both a reverence of
his majesty, with a fear of incurring his displeasure,
and at the same time a joy in his love and grace, and
an entire complacency in his beauty and bounty,
and that benignity of his which is better than life.

Our affections toward God must correspond
with the discoveries he has made of himself to us.
As he has proclaimed his name for our instruction,
so we must proclaim it to *his praise.* Now in God
there is both every thing that is awful, and every
thing that is amiable; and in his manifestations of
himself he seems to have taken a delight in put-
ting these together, and setting the one over against
the other. When he makes himself known in his
greatness, *as riding on the heavens, by his name*

1 Psalm 101:1.

JAH, he adds, in the next words, this instance of his goodness, that he is a *Father of the fatherless, and a Judge for the widows*.[1] Is he the high and lofty One that inhabits eternity, and dwells in the holy place?[2] Yet we must know that with *this* man he will dwell, to *this* man he will look, that is of a contrite and humble spirit.[3] And on the other hand, when he tells us how gracious he is in forgiving iniquity, transgression, and sin,[4] he tells us presently how just he is also, that he will by no means clear the impenitently guilty.

Thus, therefore, must we have an eye to him, both as he is infinitely great, and greatly to be feared, and as he is infinitely good, and greatly to be loved. And as no *love* one degree short of *perfect* must *cast out all fear;*[5] so no fear, in those who have received the Spirit of adoption, must damp the *delight* which, as children, we must have in *our Father*.[6] We must both fear God's name, and love it; both fear the commandment, and love it. We must delight ourselves always in the Lord; and yet we must make him our fear and our dread,[7] and be in the fear of him every day, and all the day long.

1 Psalm 68:4, 5.
2 Isaiah 57:15.
3 Isaiah 66:1, 2.
4 Exodus 34:6, 7.
5 1 John 4:18.
6 Psalm 37:4.
7 Isaiah 8:13.

In the duties of religious worship, we must know our disparity; and in consideration of that we must serve him with reverence and godly fear,[1] because God, even our God, though he be a rejoicing light to those who serve him faithfully, yet he is a consuming fire to those who trifle with him: but we must also know our privilege, and draw near to him in full assurance of faith, and must serve the Lord with gladness.[2]

2. We must keep up both a *trembling for sin*, and a *triumphing in Christ*, as the *propitiation for sin*. We must be afraid of the curse, and the terrors of it, and yet must rejoice in the covenant, and the riches and graces of it. With one eye we must look at the fiery serpents, and see what danger we are in by our having been stung by them; but with the other eye we must look up to the brazen serpent[3] lifted up on the pole, and see what a fair way we are in of being helped and healed by looking to it. *Look unto me* (saith Christ) *and be ye saved.*

We must not so look upon the comforts of the gospel, as to forget the condemnation of the law, and that we are guilty before God, and liable to that condemnation: which we must be ever mindful of, that we may daily reflect with regret upon sin, and may be quickened to flee from the wrath to come,

1 Hebrews 12:28.
2 Hebrews 10:22.
3 John 3:14.

and to flee for refuge to the hope set before us; and that knowing the terrors of the Lord, we may be persuaded to stand in awe and not sin. And yet we must not so look upon the condemnation of the law, as to forget that we are under grace, and not under the law;[1] and that we have a Redeemer to rejoice in, and with an entire confidence to rely upon, who died to save his people from their sins. We must look upon sin, and be humbled, and be afraid of God's wrath; but at the same time we must look upon Christ, and be satisfied, and hope in his mercy.

3. We must keep up both *a jealousy of ourselves,* and of our own sincerity; and a *grateful thankful sense of God's grace in us*, and the workings of that grace. It is true, the heart of man is deceitful above all things,[2] and in nothing more so than in its judgment of itself. We are all apt to be partial in our own favors; to say *we are rich and increased with goods*, when we do not know, or will not own, that we are wretched and miserable.[3] We have therefore reason to fear lest we should be mistaken, lest our graces should prove counterfeit, and we should be rejected as hypocrites at last. And O that those who live a carnal, worldly, sensual life, under the disguise of a religious profession, were awakened to see their mistake before the flames of hell awaken them! O that fearfulness

---

1 Romans 6:14.

2 Jeremiah 17:9.

3 Revelation 3:17.

would surprise those who, indeed, are hypocrites; and that the sinners in Zion were afraid; and that their vain hopes, which are built upon the sand, might be taken down before they are thrown down!

But let not those who fear the Lord, and obey the voice of his servant, walk in darkness, but trust in the name of the Lord, *and* stay themselves upon their God.[1] Let not those who, through grace, are brought to prefer the favor of God before the smiles of the world, and are more in care about the things that relate to the soul and eternity, than about those that have reference only to the body and time; let not their godly jealousy over themselves run into an extreme. Let them not be upon all occasions arraigning their evidences, and questioning, *Is the Lord among us, or is he not?* Hearken to this, you that tremble at God's word, and are fearing continually every day.[2] How can you say you do not love God, when you cannot but say that you would not for all the world wilfully offend him, and that there is nothing you desire so much as to be in his favor, and in communion with him? And therefore, though you have no reason to trust in your own merit, yet you have a great deal of reason to hope in that mercy of God, which accepts the willingness of the spirit, and overlooks the weakness of the flesh.[3]

1 Isaiah 50:10.

2 Isaiah 51:13.

3 Matthew 26:41.

Why should you wrong yourselves by bearing false witness against yourselves; as they do who make themselves poor, and yet have great riches?[1] And why should you wrong God, by robbing him of the honor of what he has wrought for you? It is true, we must not be proud of our graces, but we must be thankful for them; we must not pretend to justify ourselves to the covenant of innocency, for we are not innocent; yet we must not therefore reject the advantages of the covenant of grace, nor put from us the comforts that thence flow.

4. We must keep up both a *constant caution over our goings*, and a *constant confidence in the grace of God*. When we consider how weak we are; how apt to stumble in the way, and wander out of it, apt to tire, and apt to turn aside; we shall see cause enough to walk humbly with God. And yet, when we consider how the promises of divine aids are adapted to our case in all the exigences of it, how rich, how sure they are, and how certainly made good to all those who depend upon them, and by faith derive strength and wisdom from them, we shall see cause enough to walk boldly with God. He who walks uprightly,[2] walks with a good assurance, and may travel in the greatness of the strength of him who is mighty to save.

We have need to stand always upon our guard;

---

1 Proverbs 13:7.
2 Proverbs 10:9.

as knowing that our way lies through an enemy's country, where we have reason to expect that ambushes will be laid for us, and all the stratagems of war made use of to do us mischief. We have need to look well to our goings, and never so much as to *feed ourselves without fear,*[1] lest our *table* should *become a snare;*[2] nor walk abroad without trembling, lest under the green grass there should be a snake; lest for want of watchfulness we should be surprised by a sudden temptation, for want of resolution we should be overpowered by a violent temptation. *Happy is the man* who thus *feareth always,*[3] as seeing himself never out of the reach, no, nor ever out of the way of Satan's temptations, till he comes to heaven.

But still in the midst of this fear we must hope in God's mercy, that he will take our part against our spiritual enemies, will watch over us for good, will preserve our souls from sin, from every evil work, the only thing that can do them any real damage. What Christ said to St. Paul, when he was buffeted by a messenger of Satan, he has said to all who, like him, fly to the mercy of God, and continue instant in prayer: *My grace is sufficient for thee,*[4] though thou hast no strength of thy own that is so.

---

1 Jude 12.
2 Psalm 69:22.
3 Proverbs 28:14.
4 2 Corinthians 12:9.

Infinite Wisdom knows what grace thy case calls for; and thou shalt have enough to secure the life and happiness of thy soul, from every thing that aims at its death and ruin. Be strong therefore in the Lord, and in the power of his might;[1] go forth, and go on, in his name; as David against Goliath; and be assured that the God of peace, the God of *your* peace, will, in order to that, be the God of *your victory;* he will tread Satan under your feet, will do it shortly, will do it effectually, that he may be to eternity the God of *your triumphs.*

5. We must keep up both a *holy fear lest we come short*, and a *good hope that through grace we shall persevere*. If we rightly understand ourselves, we cannot but be often looking forward, and considering what will be our last end, what will be our future state. And what will it be? Will *our end* be peace? Will *our endless* condition be a happy one?

Truly when we look upon the brightness of the crown set before us, and our own meanness and unworthiness; when we look upon the many difficulties that lie in our way, and our own weakness, and utter inability to break through them; we may justly be afraid, lest some time or other we be guilty of a fatal miscarriage, and perish at last. And such a fear as this is recommended to us as a means to keep us from apostasy, that we may not really come short, as the unbelieving Israelites did of Canaan:

1 Ephesians 6:10.

Let us fear lest, a promise being left us of enter-ing into his rest, any of us should seem to come short,[1] should do any thing that looks like, or tends towards, a drawing back to Egypt again. We have no reason to be secure; many who thought they stood, stood as high, stood as firm as we, yet have fallen, have fallen fatally and irrecoverably. Let us, therefore, who think we stand, take heed lest we fall,[2] and with a holy fear and trembling[3] let us be continually working out our salvation. *Vigilantibus non dormientibus succurrit lex—The vigilant, not the negligent, are favored by the law.*

Yet let not this fear degenerate into amaze-ment, nor take off our chariot wheels, or make us drive heavily. While we fear lest God should leave us to ourselves, and put us into the hand of our own counsels, as justly he might, and then we are undone, let us hope in his mercy, that having begun a good work in us he will perform it. If it be the work of his own hands he will not forsake it, nay, he will perfect it, if it be indeed that which truly con-cerns us.[4] The same apostle who bids us fear lest we come short, bids us give diligence to a full assurance of hope unto the end;[5] for *faithful is he that has*

---

1 Hebrews 4:1.
2 1 Corinthians 10:12.
3 Philippians 2:12.
4 Psalm 138:8.
5 Hebrews 6:11.

called us, faithful is he that has promised, who will perform his promise, and perfect his call. To him, therefore, let us commit the keeping of our souls in well doing, the greatest trust to the best trustee; and then let it be our comfort that we *know whom we have trusted*, even one who *is able to keep what we have committed to him against that day*,[1] when it shall be called for.

Thus you see how in the great concerns of our souls there is occasion both for hope and fear, and each have their work to do, so that the two extremes of presumption and despair, those dangerous rocks, may be avoided. This is the levelling work by which the way of the Lord is to be prepared: by a good hope, every valley shall be exalted, and by a holy fear, every mountain and hill shall be brought low.[2] And thus the glory of the Lord being revealed, all flesh shall see it together.

II. The balance must likewise be kept even between hope and fear, as to our *temporal concerns,* about which we cannot be wholly unconcerned. Many cares we have upon our hearts about our life, health, ease, and safety; about our callings and estates, and the prosperity of them; our reputation and interest among men; our relations and families, and our comfort in them: all these we hold between hope and fear, and must take heed, that when

1 2 Timothy 1:12.
2 Isaiah 40:3, 4.

things look ever so hopeful we be not rocked asleep in security; and when they look ever so frightful, we do not faint away in despondency.

1. When the world smiles upon us, and our affairs in it prosper, yet then we must keep up a holy fear, and not be too confident in our pleasing prospects; not flatter ourselves with hopes of the great advancement and long continuance of our peace and prosperity; but balance the hopes which sense suggests, with the fears which reason and religion will suggest. When our bodies are in health, and we are in our full strength, the breasts full of milk, and the bones moistened with marrow;[1] when our relations are all agreeable, and such as we could wish; when our affairs are in a good posture, the trade growing, the credit firm, and every thing running in our favor; yet even then we must fear God, and the turns of his providence against us, remembering that in such as fear him he takes pleasure.

Let us not say at such a time, as David said in his prosperity,[2] *I shall never be moved, my mountain stands so strong*, that nothing can stir it, nothing shake a state of health so confirmed, a reputation so established; or as Job said in his prosperity, *I shall die in my nest, and multiply my days as the sand;*[3] or as Babylon in the height of her grandeur,

---

1 Job 21:24.

2 Psalm 30:6.

3 Job 29:18.

I shall be a lady for ever,[1] *I sit as a queen, and shall see no sorrow.*[2] Let us never promise ourselves, that because this day smiles upon us, tomorrow must needs be as this day, and much more abundant;[3] since we know not what shall be on the morrow, nor what one day may bring forth. Let us not put the evil day far from us, which for ought we know may be very near, and at the door. But, to prevent the security we are in danger of falling into at such a time.

(1.) Let us keep up an awful regard to the sovereignty of the Divine Providence, and its disposals of us and ours. We are in its hands, as clay is in the hand of the potter,[4] to be formed, unformed, new formed, as he pleases. That which seemed designed for a vessel of honor, is either marred, or with one turn of the wheel made a despised vessel, in which there is no pleasure: and shall we say, dare we say, *Why hast thou made me thus?* May not God do what he will with his own creature? and shall he not fulfil his own counsel, *whether we refuse, or whether we choose?*[5] for we are sure he is debtor to no man.

Whatever we have, it was God who gave it us;

---

1 Isaiah 47:7.
2 Revelation 18:7.
3 Isaiah 56:12.
4 Jeremiah 18:4, 6.
5 Job 34:33.

and we said when we had it, *Blessed be the name of the Lord*,[1] who in a way of sovereignty gave that to us, which he denied to others more deserving: and whatever we lose, it is God who takes it away; and when it is gone, we must say, *Blessed be the name of the Lord*, who in a way of sovereignty takes from us that which he had given us, and does us no wrong; for we are but tenants at will of all our enjoyments, even of life itself, and may be turned out at less than an hour's warning, for our times are in God's hands, not in our own.

It is true, that godliness has the promise of the life that now is; but we must take heed of misunderstanding those promises which relate to temporal good things, which are all made with this implicit proviso, *As far as is for God's glory and our good;* and further than those, if we love either God or ourselves, we shall not desire them. It is promised, that it shall be well with them that fear God; but it is not promised that they shall be always rich and great in the world, always in health, and at ease. It is promised, that no evil shall befall them, nothing that shall do them any real hurt; but it is not promised that no affliction shall befall them, for there may be need, that for a season they should be in heaviness, and it shall be for their advantage.

(2.) Let us keep up a full conviction of the vanity of this world, and the uncertainty of all our

1 Job 1:21.

enjoyments in it. We are very unapt scholars, if we have not learned, even by our own experience and observation, that there are no pleasures here below that are lasting, but they are all dying things; and that often proves least safe that is most dear. They are as flowers which will soon fade, and the sooner for being much smelled to; as snow which will soon melt, and the sooner for being taken up in our hands, and laid in our bosoms. The things we dote so much upon make themselves wings[1] (though we should not by our own improvidence and prodigality make them wings) and flee away as an eagle towards heaven. And shall we then set our eyes and hearts upon things that are not, the fashion of which passeth away, and we with it?

The things we are so fond of, we call good things, though if we have not grace to use them well, and to do good with them, they are to us good for nothing. But the Scripture calls them *deceitful riches*, and the *mammon of unrighteousness*, because they put a cheat upon those who depend upon them, and trust in them; they are not what they seem, perform not what they promise, nor last so long as one would think they should. What God has graciously promised us in them, they do perform, but not what we foolishly promise ourselves from them: so that if we are deceived, we may thank ourselves; it is our own fault for trusting to them. They perish in the

1 Proverbs 23:5.

using,[1] much more in the abusing. Let those, therefore, who are rich in this world, receive the apostle's charge, not to trust in uncertain riches, because they are uncertain; nor to lay up their treasure in them, because our estates as well as our bodies are subject, both to diseases, for *moth and rust corrupt* them, and to disasters, for *thieves break through and steal them*. What assurance can we have of, what confidence can we put in, those goods, which may be lost in an instant by the firing of a house, or the foundering of a ship at sea, by the unsuspected fraud of those we deal with, or the overpowering force of those we contend with? How can we call that *our own*, which is so much in *others' hands*, or think to hold *that* fast; when even that which is *in our hand* slips through our fingers like dust, especially if we *grasp it hard*.

(3.) Let us keep up an humble sense of our own undeservings and ill-deservings. We shall see a great deal of reason not to be confident of the continuance of our creature-comforts, when we consider that we are not worthy of the least[2] of them, no, not of the crumbs that fall from the table of common providence; and if we were not worthy to have them, much less are we worthy to have them long, and to have them secured to us. Nay, we have forfeited them all a thousand times by our abuse of

---

1 Colossians 2:22.

2 Genesis 32:10.

them; and God might justly take the forfeiture. He who is in debt is continually in fear, lest all he has be suddenly seized on: it is our case; we are in debt to the justice of God, and what can we expect, but to be stripped of all?

We had been so long ago, if God had dealt with us according to our sins; so that we have lived all our days upon forfeited favors, which therefore we can have no assurance of the continuance of.

Though we have the testimony of our consciences for us, that what we have we have got honestly, and not by fraud and oppression; and that we have used it charitably, and in some measure honored God with it, which is the likeliest way both to secure it and to increase it; yet even then we must not be secure, for God has seen that amiss in us, which we have not seen in ourselves; and there is none who can say, *I have made my heart clean, I am pure from sin.* We have all contracted guilt enough, to justify God in depriving us of all our comforts in this world; and, therefore, have no reason to be confident of the continuance of them, but a great deal of reason, whatever we lose, to say, *The Lord is righteous.*

(4.) Let us keep up a lively expectation of troubles and changes in this changeable, troublesome world. It is what we are bid to count upon, and can look for no other in a wilderness. *Time and chance happen to all;* why then should they not happen to us? The *race is not* sure *to the swift,* nor *the battle to the strong*, no, nor so much as *bread to the wise*, much less *riches to men of understanding*, or *favor to men of skill*.[1] Why then should we think them sure to us? Can you and I imagine that the world should be more kind and more constant to us, than it has been to those who went before us? You have read the story of Job, whom the rising sun saw the richest of all the men of the East, but the setting sun left poor, to a proverb. You have in your own time seen those who were once worth thousands, so reduced that they and theirs have wanted necessary food: and what exemption can we pretend to from the common calamities of human life? We are not better than our fathers, nor better than our predecessors. Shall we think our prosperity more firm than that of others has been? We might as well think that the earth should be forsaken for us, and the rock removed out of its place.

Nay, troubles and changes are good for us, they are necessary for us; the temper, or rather the distemper, of our minds make them so, lest we grow proud and secure, and in love with this world. We read of those who have no changes, and therefore they fear not God; who are not in trouble as other men,[2] and therefore pride compasses them about as a chain.[3] Moab has been at ease from his

---

1 Ecclesiastes 9:11.

2 Psalm 55:19.

3 Psalm 73:5, 6.

youth,[1] and has not by changes and troubles been emptied from vessel to vessel; and therefore he is *settled on his lees*, is grown secure and sensual, he is unhumbled and unreformed, *his taste remains in him, and his scent is not changed*. We have therefore reason to expect that God will in love to us exercise us with crosses and afflictions, that he may remind us what we are, and what we have done amiss, may wean us from this world, and draw out our thoughts and affections toward that world, the comforts of which know no changes.

(5.) Let us keep up serious thoughts of death approaching, and of our speedy removal to another world. Though the comforts we enjoy should not be taken from us, though we were ever so sure they should not, yet we know not how soon we may be taken from them, and then, how long soever they may last, they are ours no longer. Do we not perceive how frail our nature is? Are we not in deaths often, in deaths always, in death even in the midst of life? Do we not see ourselves, wherever we are, standing upon the brink of eternity, and our souls continually in our hands? And what good have we then to look for in this world, who are hastening apace out of it, and can carry nothing away with us? *What is our strength that we should hope?*[2] If we wait for a larger and finer house than what we

1 Jeremiah 48:11.
2 Job 6:11.

now live in upon earth, before it falls to us perhaps the grave may be our house, and we may make our bed in the darkness. And when our days are past, with them our purposes are broken off, even the thoughts of our heart; we and our hope go down together to the bars of the pit, when our rest is in the dust.[1]

Death will put a period to all our hopes in this world, and to all our enjoyments: how loose therefore should we sit to them, when life itself hangs so loose! He who said, *Soul, take thine ease, thou hast goods laid up for many years, eat, drink, and be merry*, was by this proved a fool, that *that* very night his *soul* was by death *required of him;*[2] and then *whose shall all these things be* which he has *provided*, and promised himself so much from? None of his we may be sure. Let us therefore be so wise as to consider our latter end, and be daily mindful of it, and then we shall not be such fools as to rely upon any thing in this world for a portion and happiness: we see we have here no continuing city, let us therefore seek and look for one that is to come.[3]

Let me now press this caution upon those whose hopes are most apt to rise high from this world, that in order to the keeping of the balance even, they

1 Job 17:11, 13, 16.
2 Luke 12:19, 20.
3 Hebrews 13:14.

may maintain a holy fear, and not grow secure:

[1.] You who are young, and setting out in the world, must be reminded not to expect great things in it. You hope you shall do as well as the best: but it may prove otherwise, that you may fare in it as ill as the worst. You are apt to look at the things of the world through that end of the perspective glass that magnifies them, and to count upon having every thing to your mind, as if there were nothing but prizes in the world's lottery; and so lay a foundation for the greater grief in the disappointment, when whatever prizes others may have, you, perhaps, may have nothing but blanks to your share: and then it will be *folly* "to curse your stars," (as some profanely speak) but *justice* to reproach yourselves for building so high on a sandy foundation, and promising yourselves satisfaction of spirit, in that which you were many a time told had nothing in it but vanity and vexation of spirit. Think not too well of yourselves, for then you are apt to prognosticate nothing but good to yourselves; but lay yourselves low, and then you will lay your expectations low.

[2.] You who are rich, and have abundance of the world, do not make that abundance *your strong city,* and a *high wall;*[1] for it is not so really, but only in your own conceit, and you may soon find it as a *bowing wall*, and a *tottering fence;* a broken reed, which will not only fail under you, but will run into

1 Proverbs 18:11.

your hand and pierce it. Keep up such a fear of God and his providence, as may forbid you ever to say unto the gold, *Thou art my hope;*[1] and to the fine gold, *Thou art my confidence;* for *if the Lord do not help you*, much more if he turn to be your enemy, and fight against you, whence can the world help you, *out of the barn-floor, or out of the winepress,*[2] out *of the farms*, or out *of the merchandise?*

[3.] You who are cheerful and gay, and cast away care, who walk in the way of your heart, and in the sight of your eyes, and withhold not yourselves from any joy, let the fear of God be a check to your mirth, and restrain it from growing into an excess. You may perhaps take care that in laughter your hearts shall not be sad,[3] but the end of this mirth may be heaviness before you are aware. When you rejoice in hope of the glory of God, that hope will not make you ashamed; but when you rejoice in hope of the wealth, and pomp, and pleasures of this world, you have *now* reason to be ashamed that you place your happiness in such things, and will *at length* be ashamed that you looked for so much from them. You are but *girding on* the harness, and therefore boast not, as though you had *put it off;*[4] *be not high-minded, but fear;* and look for *that,*

---

1 Job 31:21.

2 2 Kings 6:27.

3 Proverbs 14:13.

4 1 Kings 20:11.

every day, which may come any day.

2. When the world frowns upon us, and we are crossed, and disappointed, and perplexed in our affairs, then we must keep up a good hope, and not be inordinately cast down, no, not in our *melancholy* prospects, about our health, our safety, our name, our relations, and our effects in the world. We must not at any time burden ourselves with distracting care, what we shall eat, and what we shall drink, and wherewithal we shall be clothed;[1] but cast this care upon God, and depend upon him to care for us.[2] We must not in the worst of times torment ourselves with amazing fear, as if every thing that threatens us must needs ruin us, and every fresh gale would be a storm presently; and as if every mole-hill of difficulty in our way were an insuperable mountain. How black soever things look, and how low soever we are brought, we must not allow ourselves in fearing more than there is cause, nor more than is meet; we must not frighten ourselves with the creatures of our own imagination, nor suffer our fears to disquiet our minds, and deprive us of the government and enjoyment of ourselves, to damp our joy in God, to disturb our communion with him, and discourage our dependence on him.

But when fear weighs down the balance on that side, let us endeavor to keep it even, to keep it from

1 Matthew 6:26.
2 1 Peter 5:7.

sinking into despair, by maintaining a holy confidence in God, even as to our outward affairs: and when we are warned to *get ready for the worst,* we must still *hope the best;* hope that things are not so bad as they seem to be, that they will not be so bad as they are feared to be; and that in due time they will be better than they are. And let this hope keep our head above water, when we are ready to sink into despair; let it enable us to check ourselves for being cast down and disquieted;[1] for as bad as things are, if we *hope in God,* we shall *yet praise him.*

(1.) Hope in God's power: be fully assured of this, that how imminent soever the danger is, he can prevent it; how great soever the straits are, he can extricate us out of them, can find out a way for us in an untracked wilderness, and open springs of water to us in a dry and barren land: for with him *nothing* is *impossible,* nor is his *arm* ever *shortened,* nor his wisdom nonplused. Let us honor God, by a firm belief of his omnipotence; *Lord, if thou wilt thou canst make me whole, thou canst make me clean,* thou canst raise me up from a low estate, and raise up friends for me when I am most forlorn; by trusting in him as a God all-sufficient when creatures fail, and whom we may rejoice in as the God of our salvation, though the fig-tree do not blossom, and there be no fruit in the vine. The

---

1 Psalm 42:5.

murmuring Israelites did not in any thing affront
God so much as in saying, *Can God furnish a table
in the wilderness?*[1] *Can he give bread also?* As if any
thing was too hard for the Lord.

(2.) Hope in his providence; and believe not only
that he *can* do *any thing*, but that he *does* do *every
thing;* and whatever the event is, God does therein
perform the thing that is appointed for us,[2] and
takes cognizance of us and our affairs, how mean
and despicable soever we are. The great God has all
hearts in his hand, their hearts particularly that you
have dealings with and dependence on. The ships
on board of which your effects are, though they
are *afar off upon the sea*, are under God's eye; and
he is the confidence of *all the ends of the earth,*[3]
the remotest plantations where your concerns lie.
And shall not that God who governs the world, be
intrusted with the disposal of your concerns?

Hope in the *usual method* of Providence, which
sets prosperity and adversity *one over against the
other;* and when the ebb is at the lowest makes the
tide to turn, and the day to dawn when the night
is at the darkest. It is the glory of Providence to
help the helpless, to raise the poor out of the dust,
and bring back even from the gates of death; to
breathe upon dry bones, and say unto them, *Live.*

---

1 Psalm 78:19.

2 Job 25:14.

3 Psalm 65:5.

Let this encourage us to hope, that when things are at the worst they will mend; and therefore, as in the heights of prosperity we must rejoice as though we rejoiced not, so in the depths of adversity we must weep as though we wept not; *non si male, nunc et olim, sic erit—not as though, because circumstances have been and are adverse, they are ever to remain so.* God generally comforts his people, according to the time that he has afflicted them.[1]

(3.) Hope in his pity and tender compassions; which in the day of your grief and fear, you are to look upon yourselves as the proper objects of. The text directs us particularly to hope in his mercy; we must depend upon the goodness of his nature for that which we have not an express promise for. Let this silence our fear, that the God in whose hand our times are, is gracious and merciful, does not afflict willingly, nor grieve the children of men, much less his own children, but when there is cause, and when there is need, and therefore will not always chide, will not contend for ever; but though he cause grief, he will have compassion.[2] We may with a good assurance *fall into the hands of the Lord,* (and whose hands soever we fall into, they are *his* hands) for we know that his mercies are great, and those who hope in them shall find them so.

(4.) Hope in his promise; that word of his upon

1 Psalm 90:15.
2 Lamentations 3:31, 32.

which he hath caused us to hope, and which we have all the reason in the world to build upon,[1] for not one *iota* or tittle of it shall fall to the ground. Though he has not promised to deliver us from that *particular* evil we have a dread of, or to give us that *particular* comfort and success we are desirous of, yet he has promised that nothing shall harm them who are followers of him; nay, that all things shall work together for good to them;[2] and (which is enough to silence all our fears) that though our calamities may separate us from the dearest comfort and comforters we have in this world, yet they shall never be able to separate us from the love of God, which is in Christ Jesus our Lord,[3] from divine comforts, and the divine Comforter.

And now, who is there here that stands in need of this caution against despondency of spirit under discouraging events, and to whom it is seasonable to recommend a believing hope for the balancing and silencing of their distrustful fears? Let them apply this to themselves, and make use of the hope recommended to them as an anchor of the soul,[4] to keep them steady in a storm.

[1.] You who are beginning the world with fear and trembling, who are humble, and honest, and

---

1 Psalm 119:49.

2 1 Peter 3:13.

3 Romans 8:39.

4 Hebrews 6:19.

diligent, but have little to begin with, have many difficulties to break through, and are very diffident of your own understanding; be not discouraged, but hope in God's mercy. Your friends are few, unable to help you, or unkind and regardless of you; father and mother have perhaps forsaken you.[1] Know then that you are the particular care of Providence, which gathers the outcasts, and provides even for young ravens, when they are deserted. *Trust in the Lord*, therefore, *and do good*, so *shalt thou dwell in the land;* and though thou be not feasted, yet *verily thou shalt be fed.*[2] Though the beginning be small, the latter end may by the blessing of God greatly increase,[3] and a little one may become a thousand.

[2.] You who have concerns that lie at hazard, in danger at sea, or of being a prey to the enemy; who have debts in bad hands, or dear relations that you have dependence upon, or delight in, in peril; give not way to amazing fear, that fear which has torment, but hope in God's mercy. Give not up any thing for gone, till it is gone: and when it is gone, yet give not up all for gone, as long as you have the good providence of God to trust to. Say not, as David in his haste, *I am cast out of thy sight*, or, *I shall one day perish by the hand of Saul;* but wait on the Lord, and be of good courage, resolved to

---

1 Psalm 27:10.

2 Psalm 32:3.

3 Job 8:7.

welcome his holy will, whatever it be. We are sometimes told that the merchants are *in pain* for such a
ship, such a fleet; you think at such a time, it is only
the news of their safe arrival that will put you out
of your pain. And what if that news never come?
then you condemn yourselves to a lasting uneasi-
ness. But let me recommend that to you, which will
make you easy, whatever the event be; commit your
way to God, by a believing prayer, and submit your
will to God by a penitent resignation; and then let
your thoughts be established.

[3.] You who, by the providence of God, are
from fullness reduced to straits, have met with
losses which you think can never be repaired, and
conclude you shall never see a good day again, but
are undone to all intents and purposes; do not give
way to these desponding thoughts, but hope in the
mercy of God, that mercy which brings low, and
raises up. As Job's troubles are a warning to those
in prosperity not to be secure, so his return to his
former splendor, is a warning to those in adversity
not to despair. You know not what better times you
may yet be reserved for, as Job was, whose latter end
God blessed more than his beginning.[1]

III. I come now briefly to show how the balance must be kept even between hope and fear as to
public concerns, both those of the church abroad,
and of our own nation. Are not the concerns of the

1 Job 42:12.

church abroad our concerns? They ought to be so.
I hope we all lay them near our hearts, as mem-
bers of the great body, and hearty well-wishers to
its interests, and to the honor and kingdom of its
great Head. Are we not in care that the Christian
religion may get ground among men, and not lose
the ground it has; that it may prevail and rule in its
power and purity; that the bounds of the church
may be enlarged by the accession both of Jews and
Gentiles to it; that the breaches of it may be healed,
by the pouring out of a spirit of love and charity
upon all who belong to it; that the ordinances of
Christ, administered according to the institution of
them, may ever be its glory, and upon that glory
there may ever be a defense; a cloud created by day,
and the shining of a flaming fire by night, both
upon every dwelling place of Mount Zion, and
upon her assemblies?[1]

The land of our nativity ought in a particular
manner to be dear to us, for in the peace or trouble of that, we have peace[2] or trouble. Is it not our
concern, that our liberty and property be secured;
that the government flourish; that the public peace
and tranquillity be continued; that justice be duly
administered; that the power and influence of
the nation abroad be advanced; that the trade be
protected and increased; but, above all, that the

1 Isaiah 4:5.
2 Jeremiah 29:7.

protestant religion be transmitted pure to those who shall come after us; that the bulwarks erected against popery may be strengthened; that atheism, infidelity, and all iniquity, may be made to stop their mouth; that the form of godliness may ever be the beauty of the nation, and the power of it may ever rule in men's hearts and lives? Is it not our concern, that our eyes should still see our teachers, and that they should not again be removed into corners, nor our religious assemblies broken up and scattered? If it be, we cannot but look forward with concern, and while we enjoy peace and liberty at present, be in care about the continuance of them; and in our prospects there cannot but be a mixture of hope and fear, and we must endeavor so to fear the worst, as not to grow secure, and so to hope the best, as not to despond, or be dispirited.

The truth is, we are very apt at some times, when second causes smile a little, to be very sanguine, above what there is reason for, and to conclude, that we shall without fail be in Canaan presently; at other times, when things go not just to our mind, we are apt to be very chagrined, more than there is cause, and to conclude that we shall without remedy be hurried back into Egypt again. This hour we soar, and if the wind turn, next hour we sink; as if when the sun shines we should think it would never rain, and when it rains we should think the sun would never shine out again. And have we not lived long enough in this world to be ashamed both of those hopes and those fears? having often seen ourselves disappointed both in the one and the other; and in the issue things have proved neither so well as we hoped, nor so ill as we feared; so that we have surely at length learned by experience, that it is our wisdom and interest, as well as our duty, to keep the balance even between hope and fear.

1. We have always reason to keep up a holy fear as to public affairs, and to be apprehensive of trouble before us, even when things look most promising. We have no reason, even when we dwell peaceably, as the men of Israel in Solomon's time, to dwell carelessly, as the men of Laish.[1] It is true, and we have a great deal of reason to be thankful for it, that we are a happy people; we have long been blessed with peace and plenty at home, and with victory and success abroad; we live under a very good government, which seeks the welfare of our people, speaking peace to all their seed; we have long sitten every one under his own vine, and under his own fig-tree; we have long enjoyed the free exercise of our religion, and great plenty of the means of grace, and there has been none to make us afraid. Our fleece has been wet with the dews of heaven, when that of other nations has been dry: while theirs also has been wet with showers of blood, ours has been dry.

1 Judges 18:7.

Shall England then say, *I sit as a queen, and shall see no sorrow?* By no means. Happy is the man that still feareth, as David, whose flesh trembled for fear of God;[1] and notwithstanding the many mercies he had received from him, was afraid of his judgments. And we have reason to be so; for,

(1.) We are a provoking people. Atheism and profaneness abound among us, notwithstanding the testimonies borne against them, and the endeavors used to suppress them. Vice is become fashionable and epidemical; all flesh have corrupted their way; *the whole head sick, the whole heart faint.*[2] How is God's name dishonored, his day profaned, his good creatures abused to luxury and excess; and how does the unclean spirit range through the land! Liberty to sin has been pleaded for as *Christian liberty*, and the societies for reformation branded as *illegal inquisitions*, and their pious endeavors opposed, insulted, and ridiculed. And shall not God visit for these things? *Shall not his soul be avenged on such a nation as this?*[3] How can a people who hate to be reformed, hope to be saved?

The great decay of serious godliness among those who run not with others to an excess of riot, is likewise a very threatening symptom. If those grow more insolent who are filling the measure of the

1 Psalm 119:120.

2 Isaiah 1:5.

3 Jeremiah 9:9.

nation's guilt by their wickedness, and at the same time those grow more cold and remiss, who should empty it by their prayers and tears, things look very ill indeed. How woefully do the professors of this age degenerate from the zeal and strictness of their predecessors! And such is the corruption of the rising generation in many families, that there is reason to fear a further degeneracy. And if thus we grow worse and worse, what will become of us at last? If thus, as Ezra speaks, the holy seed mingle themselves with, and conform themselves to, the people of these abominations, what may we expect, but that God should be angry with us till he hath consumed us?[1] For our religion sensibly consumes, and a consumption may be as fatal as a stab. Those may be of any religion, who are of no religion.

(2.) We are a divided people, and our divisions give just cause to fear the worst; for what can be expected, but that a kingdom divided against itself should be brought to desolation? It is our enemies' policy to divide us, and our sin and folly to serve their design by our misunderstandings one of another, and disaffection one to another, when we might countermine and defeat it by our mutual love and charity. For the divisions of our Reuben, there cannot but be great thoughts and searchings of heart among all who are concerned for the public welfare. We are in danger of being burnt up by

1 Ezra 9:2, 14.

the heats in our own bosoms, and broken to pieces by the blows we give one another; and who can we think will be our deliverers, if we be thus our own destroyers?

It is not so much the difference of sentiment that is threatening, nor the difference of practice according to that sentiment; I never expect to see all wise men of a mind, and good men will not act against their judgment; but that which does us the mischief, is the mismanagement of our differences, our uncharitable censures one of another, and reflections one upon another, our heats and animosities, and party-making, to the destruction, not only of Christian charity, but of common friendship and good neighborhood. The breach seems wide as the sea, which cannot be healed; and what will be in the end hereof? If we thus bite and devour one another, what can be expected, but that we should be consumed one of another?[1] While our enemies triumph in our divisions, it becomes us to tremble because of them.

(3.) God has told us, that in the world we shall have tribulation; all the disciples of Christ most count upon it, and not flatter themselves with hopes of an uninterrupted tranquillity any where on this side heaven. The church is here militant, its state in this world is a warfare: if it retire sometimes into quarters of refreshment, yet it must expect to

1 Galatians 5:15.

be drawn out into the field again next campaign: if it have its intervals of peace, those are intended as breathing times, that it may recruit and gather strength for an encounter with another trouble. Once we read that the land of Israel had rest fourscore years;[1] but we never read afterwards that it had so long a respite. We are in a wilderness, and we must expect to fare no better than the church in the wilderness did,[2] which though sometimes it pitched where there were twelve wells of water,[3] yet presently was where there was no water[4] to drink; and when it removed from the wilderness of Sin, the cloud that was their guide led them to the wilderness of Paran;[5] but still they were in a desert land, where God, though he led them about, yet instructed them. Let the people of God never expect, till they come to heaven, to be out of the reach of evil, and therefore never expect to be perfectly quiet from the fear of it.

Far be it from me to suggest any thing that may create disquieting jealousies: all that I aim at in mentioning these grounds of fear, is, that hereby we may all be awakened to our duty.

[1.] Let us, in consideration hereof, stir up

---

1 Judges 3:30.

2 Acts 7:38.

3 Exodus 15:27.

4 Exodus 17:3.

5 Numbers 10:12.

ourselves to pray, and to wrestle with God in prayer, for the turning away of the judgments, which our own sins, and the malice of those who are the enemies of our public peace, threaten us with. Jacob feared Esau his brother, and then prayed, *Deliver me, I pray thee*, from him.[1] Jehoshaphat feared, and then set himself to seek the Lord, and proclaim a fast.[2] Whatever are the grounds of our fear, we know God can remove them; he can turn away ungodliness from Jacob,[3] and then he comes as a Redeemer to Zion.

Let not our prayers for the church of God, and for our own nation, degenerate into a formality; nor let us grow customary in them, as if it were only for fashion' sake, that we prayed for the queen and the government, the preservation of the protestant succession, and the prosperity of the nation and its allies, and (as some vainly drink healths to these) only for a compliment. I fear lest some who join with us in prayer, however in other parts of the service they think themselves somewhat concerned, when we come to that, grow remiss and indifferent, as if that were nothing to them; whereas our Lord Jesus has taught us, before we pray for our daily bread and the pardon of our sins, to pray for the prosperity of his church, that his name may

---

1 Genesis 32:11.

2 2 Chronicles 20:3.

3 Romans 11:26.

be sanctified, his kingdom may come, and his will be done. Let us therefore not only join heartily with our ministers in prayer for the church of God, and for the nation, but let each of us in our families and closets be intercessors with God for public mercies; let us stand in the gap to turn away his wrath, and give him no rest till he establish, till he make Jerusalem a praise in the earth.[1]

[2.] Let us, in consideration hereof, do what we can to prevent the judgments that threaten us, by a personal reformation of heart and life, and by contributing what we can in our places to the reformation of others. When God speaks concerning a nation, to pluck up, and to pull down, and to destroy,[2] its turning from sin is the only way to save it from ruin, and that is a sure way. It is the *island of the innocent* that is *delivered by the pureness of their hands.*[3] Let this charity to the public begin at home. Let every Israelite, as once every Ninevite, turn from his evil way; and then who can tell but God will yet return and repent,[4] and leave a blessing behind him? But let not this charity end there; let us appear on the Lord's side; let us act in defense of injured virtue and despised godliness, and do our utmost in humility and sincerity to put vice and

---

1 Isaiah 62:6, 7.
2 Jeremiah 18:7, 8.
3 Job 22:30.
4 Jonah 3:10.

profaneness out of countenance. And if we thus return to God in a way of duty, no doubt he will return to us in a way of mercy, and be better to us than our fears.

[3.] Being warned of a deluge coming, let us provide accordingly: let not the warning make us despond and despair. Noah did not; he knew the deluge should not be a final destruction of mankind, but that there would be another world after that which was to be drowned; he knew also that it should go well with him, and his family. With this hope he encouraged himself; but being warned of God concerning it, he was moved with fear, and made provision for it; he walked with God, and they who do so are sure to be hid in the day of the Lord's anger,[1] to be hid either in heaven or under heaven. He prepared an ark, and then was himself saved in it. Christ is our ark, God has prepared in him a refuge for all those who flee to him, and take shelter in him when a deluge comes. Preserve the evidences of your interest in Christ clear and unclouded, and your hopes of eternal life firm and unshaken; lay up a treasure of comforts and experiences; make the name of the Lord your strong tower; his attributes, his promises, your sanctuary, into which you may run and be safe, in which you may rest and be easy, and, then, welcome the will of God, nothing can come amiss.

1 Zephaniah 2:3.

2. Whatever cause we may see to fear, yet still we must keep up a good hope, as to public affairs. We hear of the threatening powers and policies of our enemies, the heads and horns of the dragon,[1] that makes war with the Lamb. We see the church in many places afflicted, tossed with tempests, and not comforted; her adversaries many and mighty, her helpers few and feeble; yet let not our faith and hope fail; it is day, though it be cloudy and dark, and at evening time it shall be light.[2] Let Israel hope in God, and wait for him, as those who wait for the morning; and when the night is long and gloomy, do as Paul's mariners did, cast anchor, and wish for the day.[3] Let us learn to make the best of that which is, and hope the best concerning that which shall be.

Let our hopes always be such a check upon our fears, that they may not prevail to disturb our communion with God, to stop the mouth of prayer, and weaken the hands of honest endeavor. Hearken not to the foolish surmises of danger, nor be put into a fright by evil tidings; *Say not, A confederacy, to whom this people shall say, A confederacy; neither fear ye their fear, nor be afraid,* but *make God your fear and your dread.*[4] The more we are governed by the fear of God, the less we shall be disturbed by the

---

1 Revelation 12:3.

2 Zechariah 14:7.

3 Acts 27:29.

4 Isaiah 8:11, 12.

fear of man. Nehemiah encouraged the builders of
the wall with this, when they were surrounded with
enemies, who designed to come in the midst among
them, and slay them, and cause the work to cease.
*Be not afraid of them, remember the Lord which
is great and terrible,*[1] greater and more terrible to
them than they can be to us, and who will show
himself above them in that thing wherein they deal
proudly. When you fear continually every day, as
if the oppressor in his fury[2] were ready to destroy,
you forget the Lord your Maker, and his dominion
over all, and the dependence of every creature upon
him; which, if you had a due regard to, you would
look with contempt upon Sennacherib himself, and
would say, *Where is the fury of the oppressor?*

Let me prevail with you at this day to encourage yourselves in the Lord your God as to public affairs. While we fear our own sins, let us hope
in God's mercy; for though our iniquities prevail
against us, and threaten to stop the current of
God's favors, yet as for our transgressions he shall
purge them away,[3] and that great obstacle being
removed, his favors shall have a free course again.
Though the designs of our enemies be laid ever so
deep, and their hopes ever so high, yet God can
make even their wrath to praise him, and restrain

---

1 Nehemiah 4:11, 14.

2 Isaiah 51:13.

3 Psalm 65:3.

the remainder of it;[1] and therefore take heed and be quiet, fear not, neither be faint-hearted,[2] but hope that things will end well at last.

There are three things which may encourage our hope, and keep the balance even against all our fears, as to the concerns both of the protestant churches abroad, and our own nation.

(1.) The word which God has spoken to us; which (whatever other props our hopes may be supported with) is the great foundation on which they must be built, and then they are fixed. If our hopes be grounded on the promise, and our expectations guided by it, they are as the house built on the rock; and the heart that is supported by them is established and cannot be moved.[3] *Si fractus illabatur orbis, impavidum ferient ruinæ—Though the earth be removed, yet we will not fear.*[4] But if our hopes be founded on the ability and agency of creatures, they rise or fall as second causes smile or frown; as the ship upon the water, which is higher or lower, as the tide ebbs or flows. The stocks are as the news is, and then every turn of the wheel otherwise than we would have it, shakes our hopes, and robs us of the comfort of them. Be persuaded therefore to hope for what God had promised, according

---

1 Psalm 76:10.

2 Isaiah 7:4.

3 Psalm 112:7, 8.

4 Psalm 46:2.

to the true intent and fall extent of the promise, and because he has promised it, and that hope shall be an anchor of the soul sure and steadfast.

Is not this the word which God has spoken, and on which he hath caused us to hope? That the *kingdoms of the world shall become his kingdoms:* That *Christ shall have the heathen given him for his inheritance, and the ends of the earth shall see his salvation.* Has he not said that the *man of sin shall be consumed*, the mystery of iniquity unravelled, and that the New-Testament Babylon shall *sink like a millstone into the mighty waters?* Has he not said, that the day will come when *swords shall be beaten into ploughshares, and spears into pruninghooks*, when the *wolf and the lamb shall lie down together*, and there shall be *none to hurt or destroy in all the holy mountain?* Has he not said, that *for the oppression of the poor, and the sighing of the needy, he will arise, and set them in safety from those that puff at them?* That *the rod of the wicked shall not always rest on the lot of the righteous*, but *the year of the redeemed will come*, and the *year of recompenses for the controversy of Zion?* Has he not said, *that a seed shall serve Christ, which shall be accounted to him for a generation;* that *the name of Christ shall endure for ever;* and that *the church is built upon a rock, and the gates of hell shall never prevail against it?*

This, and a great deal more to this purpose, he

has said; and he is not a man that he should lie, nor the son of man that he should repent. Has he made the promise, and shall he not make it good? In this therefore let us trust, in this let us triumph—God has spoken in his holiness; he has given me his word for it, and then I will rejoice; I will divide Sechem, Gilead is mine, Manasseh mine:[1] it is all my own as far as the promise goes, which we must not so much as stagger at.

(2.) The work which God has begun among us. We have reason to hope in God's mercy; for the interest that lies so much upon our hearts, even the interest of religion among us, is the interest of God's own kingdom, which he has set up among us, and will therefore keep up: it is the work of his own hands,[2] which he will never forsake.

Things are not so bad, but, blessed be God, there are some hopeful, favorable symptoms in our case; and none more so, than the national testimonies that are borne against atheism and infidelity, and the threatening growth of deism, Socinianism, and scepticism among us; the complaints that are justly made of the profanation of the Lord's Day, and the contempt cast upon the Scripture and divine institutions; of the wretched corruption of manners, and the influence which the profaneness of the stage has upon it. When these things are represented as the

1 Psalm 60:6, 7.
2 Psalm 102:25.

real grievances of the nation, and lamented accordingly, surely now there is hope in Israel, concerning this thing,[1] and we may rejoice in that hope.

I trust God has among us a remnant of praying people, a remnant that hold fast their integrity; and with an eye to them God will continue to save us, and will perfect what he has wrought. We may safely argue, as Haman's wife does, for the perfecting of the ruin of our enemies; *If Mordecai be of the seed of the Jews*, if the cause be God's, as certainly it is, before whom, before which, thou hast begun to fall, thou shalt not, thou canst not prevail, though thou struggle ever so hard, but shalt surely, shalt irrecoverably, fall before him[2] and it. And we may also argue, as Manoah's wife does, for the preventing of our own ruin; *If the Lord had been pleased to kill us, he would not as at this time have showed us such things as these.*[3] As for God, his work is perfect; if he *bring to the birth, he will cause to bring forth.*[4]

(3.) The wonders which he has wrought for us. When we are encouraging ourselves with hopes that God will ordain peace for us, because he has wrought our work in us;[5] yet this is discouraging,

1 Ezra 10:2.
2 Esther 6:13.
3 Judges 13:23.
4 Isaiah 66:9.
5 Isaiah 26:12.

that there are such difficulties in the way, which we think can never be got over. But let us then consider the former times, remember the works of the Lord, and his wonders of old;[1] not only those which our fathers have told us of, but which we have seen in our own days, whereby God's work has been begun, carried on in a surprising way, and by events which we looked not for.

When God had began to deliver Israel out of Egypt, and conduct them to Canaan by miracles, he expected that in their straits they should depend upon him still to work miracles for their relief, and was displeased at their unbelief if they did not. God has begun to save us, though not by miracles, yet by marvels; and thereby has encouraged us to depend upon him that he will still do wonders for us, rather than the work he has done should be undone again. If a mean and worthless people may be saved by a divine prerogative, why may not a weak and help-less people be saved by a divine omnipotence?

Be of good courage therefore, and hope in God, that we shall yet praise him; stay yourselves upon him, strengthen yourselves in him, look upwards with cheerfulness, and then look forward with sat-isfaction. Let your hopes quicken your prayers, let them keep you in the way of duty, and enlarge your hearts to run in that way; let them quicken your endeavors in your places, to serve the interests of

1 Psalm 77:11.

God's kingdom among us to the utmost of your power; and then let them silence your fears, and make you always easy to yourselves and those about you. Comfort yourselves and one another with this, that the same almighty hand that has laid the foundations of his church among us, will build upon those foundations, will in his own way and time, in his own method, and according to the plan of his own eternal counsels, carry on the building, till at length the top-stone be brought forth with shouting, and we shall cry, *Grace, grace to it.*[1]

---

1 Zechariah 4:7.

NOTES

NOTES

MAN'S QUESTIONS & GOD'S ANSWERS

Am I accountable to God?
Each of us will give an account of himself to God. ROMANS 14:12 (NIV).

Has God seen all my ways?
Everything is uncovered and laid bare before the eyes of him to whom we must give account. HEBREWS 4:13 (NIV).

Does he charge me with sin?
But the Scripture declares that the whole world is a prisoner of sin. GALATIANS 3:22 (NIV).
All have sinned and fall short of the glory of God. ROMANS 3:23 (NIV).

Will he punish sin?
The soul who sins is the one who will die. EZEKIEL 18:4 (NIV).
For the wages of sin is death, but the gift of God is eternal life in Christ Jesus our Lord. ROMANS 6:23 (NIV).

Must I perish?
He is patient with you, not wanting anyone to perish, but everyone to come to repentance. 2 PETER 3:9 (NIV).

How can I escape?
Believe in the Lord Jesus, and you will be saved. ACTS 16:31 (NIV).

Is he able to save me?
Therefore he is able to save completely those who come to God through him. HEBREWS 7:25 (NIV).

Is he willing?
Christ Jesus came into the world to save sinners. 1 TIMOTHY 1:15 (NIV).

Am I saved on believing?
Whoever believes in the Son has eternal life, but whoever rejects the Son will not see life, for God's wrath remains on him. JOHN 3:36 (NIV).

Can I be saved now?
Now is the time of God's favor, now is the day of salvation. 2 CORINTHIANS 6:2 (NIV).

As I am?
Whoever comes to me I will never drive away. JOHN 6:37 (NIV).

Shall I not fall away?
Him who is able to keep you from falling. JUDE 1:24 (NIV).

If saved, how should I live?
Those who live should no longer live for themselves but for him who died for them and was raised again. 2 CORINTHIANS 5:15 (NIV).

What about death and eternity?
I am going there to prepare a place for you. I will come back and take you to be with me that you also may be where I am. JOHN 14:2-3 (NIV).